JAILS IN AMERICA

An Overview of Issues

Published by
The American Correctional Association
4321 Hartwick Road, Suite L-208
College Park, Maryland 20740
(301) 699-7600

In cooperation with
The National Coalition for Jail Reform
c/o School of Criminal Justice
Rutgers University
15 Washington Street
Newark, New Jersey 07102
(201) 648-5204

JAILS IN AMERICA
An Overview of Issues

is a reprint of

COVERING THE JAIL: Resources for the Media which was made possible by grants from the Chicago Resource Center and the North Shore Unitarian Universalist Veatch Program. Points of view or opinions in this document are those of the authors and do not necessarily represent the positions or policies of either grantor organization.

Originally published by the National Coalition for Jail Reform.

Preface

Although a number equal to three percent of the U.S. population will pass through the nation's 3,493 jails each year, most people know little about this community institution in their midst.

What most people think about the jail, when they think about it at all, is that it is "the place to lock up the bad guys." Yet the majority of people in jail have not been convicted of the charges for which they are held. They are simply awaiting trial, many of them too poor to post bail for their release. Others have committed only minor offenses and are being held for transfer to a social service agency.

Many jails are physically deteriorating, crowded beyond capacity not only with pretrial detainees and sentenced inmates, but also with juveniles, mentally ill and retarded people, and public inebriates for whom no other facilities or services are available. Jails are often underfunded and understaffed and a growing number are under court order to improve conditions. They face enormous and complicated problems, many of which are growing worse.

Each jail is different from all others. Each is both a reflection of the community it serves and a part of a larger criminal justice system. To understand the jail, it is necessary to look at all the diverse forces that affect it—the role of judges, county commissioners, social service agencies, the public and others.

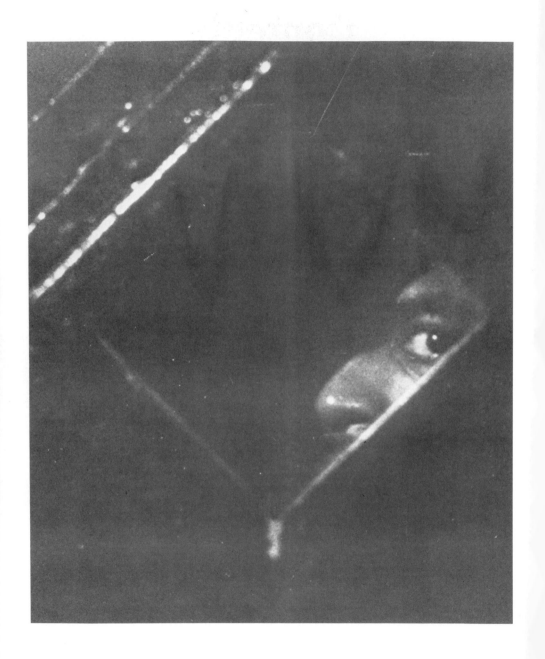

Contents

Cover Art by Michelle Morgan
Photos courtesy of National Coalition for Jail Reform

What Is A Jail?

A jail is:

- a facility administered, operated, and primarily funded by a county or city;
- a place to detain people who are awaiting trial. Detention occurs after a person has been arrested and charged, but before a trial has been held to determine guilt or innocence. These people are referred to as "pretrial detainees." They may be detained to await their first court appearance, for bail to be set and made, for trial or for release;
- used to hold people who are to be transferred to a state or federal prison;
- used to hold people who are to be transferred to a state mental hospital, alcohol or drug detoxification facility, or juvenile shelter;
- used to punish people convicted of a minor crime (usually a misdemeanor) and who have been sentenced to (usually) a year or less. The punishment in this case is deprivation of liberty by incarceration in the jail.

A jail may be known locally as a work house, stockade, house of corrections, detention center or correctional institution. In one state—Pennsylvania—jails are called prisons. Also, in six states—Delaware, Alaska, Hawaii, Rhode Island, Vermont, and Connecticut—a combined jail/prison system is operated by the state. These, however, are exceptions to the rule.

A prison is:

- not the same thing as a jail;
- a facility administered, operated, and funded by a state or the federal government;
- used to punish people convicted of more serious crimes (usually felonies) and in most states sentenced to more than a year.

Thus, the people in your local facility are "jailed," while those serving time in a state or federal institution have been "imprisoned."

1

A **lockup** is:

- a facility usually operated by police and located in police station houses or headquarters or in a separate area of the jail building;
- a temporary holding facility. Arrestees are usually held for no more than 48 hours (excluding weekends and holidays) until they are taken before a judge or released;
- used to "dry out" inebriated people;
- used to hold youths until parents can be summoned or another placement arranged.

There are more than 15,000 *lockups* in cities across the country. However, there has never been a national survey of lockups, and little information is available on their size, conditions or population. Many homeless people or people society cannot easily deal with are held in lockups and the suicide rate in lockups seems, from newspaper reports, to be very high.

B. Silverstein, courtesy of Anne Bolduc and National Institute of Corrections

This book focuses only on jails. There are 3,493 jails in the United States.

- 2,900 jails are operated by counties, the remainder by cities.
- 44 percent of the jails, usually in rural areas, hold 10 or fewer inmates each day.
- 4 percent of the jails, mostly in large metropolitan areas, hold an average of 250 or more inmates each day.
- Most jails house both men and women, but a number of larger systems have separate buildings for men and women.
- Newer jails often provide varying levels of inmate security (minimum, medium and maximum) with areas for medical care, recreation, food service, visitation, various programs and services.
- Many small rural jails consist of a few cells, an office, and one to three staff members who perform other law enforcement functions in addition to guarding inmates, transporting them to and from court, cooking their meals or bringing in food from the local fast-food carryout.
- 10 percent of the jails are under court order to improve conditions and make other changes.
- In the 1982 Bureau of Justice Statistics *Survey of Jail Inmates,* there were 209,582 people in local jails on the given day. There is considerable turnover in jail populations (as opposed to prisons where inmates are serving longer sentences). It is estimated that seven million people pass through jails each year.

Who Is In Jail?

The profile of jail inmates nationally indicates that they tend to be young, poor and undereducated, with many out of work and dependent on welfare and unemployment benefits prior to incarceration. They include an overrepresentation of minorities compared to the general population. A majority are awaiting trial and have not been found guilty of the charges for which they are held.

According to the most recent *Survey of Jail Inmates,* conducted by the Bureau of Justice Statistics, on June 30, 1982:

- 209,582 people were in jail on that day, a third higher than four years earlier.
- 7,000,000 people passed through our jails in the preceding 12 months, about three percent of the total U.S. population.
- 60 percent were awaiting arraignment or trial; they had not been convicted of the crime with which they were charged. This is an increase from 1978, when 40 percent of the people in jail were awaiting trial.
- 43 percent were convicted and serving sentences.
- 6.6 percent of the 209,582 people in jail on June 30, 1982 were women.
- 8.2 percent were juveniles.
- 47 percent were white.
- 40 percent were black.
- 12 percent were Hispanic.
- The average stay in jail was 11 days, although this represents a wide range of lengths of time.
- 40 percent of all people in jail on June 30, 1982 were held in the nation's 100 largest jails.

These figures are derived from a sample survey of jail inmates taken by the Bureau of Justice Statistics in 1982 to update data collected in its last complete census of jail inmates in 1978. A second complete census was conducted in 1983, with data published in late 1984. BJS plans to conduct complete jail censuses every five years in the future.

From the 1978 census, we find:

- 158,394 people were in jail on the census day.
- 70 percent of that total were under 30 years of age; one out of three inmates were in the 20-24 age bracket, compared to one out of seven in the general population.
- 61 percent had less than a high school education.
- 54 percent were never married.
- 43 percent had dependents, including 47 percent of the women in jail and 58 percent of the black women in jail.

Minorities and the Poor in Jail

Minorities and poor people are found in the nation's jail population in numbers disproportionate to their percentage of the general population:

- Blacks comprise only 12 percent of the U.S. population, but 40 percent of the jail population.
- Hispanics comprise only six percent of the U.S. population, but 12 percent of the jail population.
- 50 percent of the women in jail are black.

- In Alaska, the mean jail sentence received by Alaskan natives for misdemeanors is 83 percent longer than that given whites.
- 43 percent of all jail inmates were unemployed at the time of incarceration, including 66 percent of the women in jail and 71 percent of the black women in jail.
- 45 percent of all inmates had no income or less than $3,000 income during the year prior to incarceration; this figure increases to 56 percent for women inmates and 60 percent for black women inmates.
- 81 percent of all inmates and 92 percent of women inmates had no income or less than $10,000 income during the year prior to incarceration.
- The median income for all jail inmates during the year prior to incarceration was $3,714; it was $2,416 for women inmates.
- 81 percent of all unconvicted inmates had bail set, but 57 percent of those with bail set could not afford to pay it. A third of these could not afford even $125 in bail.

A Note About Jail Statistics

Local jail information and data, as with national data, are often difficult to come by. Jails are seldom required to report data to state or federal authorities. Even when local jails report population statistics to their state Departments of Corrections, there is often no uniformity of definitions, categories, or collection methods to make data from one jail comparable with other jails within the state or in another state.

Most jails have a basic information sheet on each inmate. These forms may include such data as age, sex, race, employment history, educational level, and marital status. Jails with computerized information systems may compile reports on a weekly, monthly or yearly basis which aggregate this information. In New York State, for example, every county jail administrator is required to submit a yearly report to the State Commission of Correction, summarizing the characteristics of the jail population. In other states, the only way to obtain this kind of data is to request that jail officials compile the information by sorting the basic information sheets on all inmates by hand, a tedious and time consuming process.

In addition, some jails prepare a Daily Report or Record on each inmate, containing dates of admission and release, reason for commitment, number of previous offenses, court of commitment, term of sentence and other legal information. In other communities, this information may be available from the clerk of the court. Larger urban jurisdictions may aggregate the data; in other places, they will be available only on an individual case basis.

Some jails collect extensive information about each inmate, including medical and psychiatric histories, past criminal activities, financial data, and information about personal problems. Because

5

of the need for confidentiality, this information about individuals is usually not made available to the public or the media.

Because of the large number of jails and the constantly changing population in jails, academic research has tended to concentrate on the prison population which is relatively stable, where data are collected in a more standardized way and where one needs to go to fewer sources to collect the data. Jail data have not been subject to the same kind of analysis given prison data.

What Does A Jail Cost?

As with other jail data, there is no standardized or uniform method for collecting jail cost information nationwide. Nevertheless, a number of organizations have published studies of jail costs, based on the best available information, which give a range of figures with which to work.

Jail costs are usually separated into *construction, financing* and *operating* costs.

Construction Costs

The Bureau of Justice Statistics estimates that it costs an average of $43,000 to build one bed space in a "constitutional jail," that is, a jail which would meet emerging national jail standards. BJS estimates that one bed space in a new "advanced practices jail" averages $51,000.

The National Moratorium on Prison Construction of the Unitarian Universalist Service Committee examined the costs associated with new jails proposed or under construction in early 1984. It estimated that the average cost of such a new jail will total $5.77 million and the average cost per bed space will be $49,306.

In figuring the cost of a new or remodeled jail in your community, a number of factors must be taken into consideration. The primary cost elements are:

• Construction
• Site acquisition and preparation
• Furnishings and equipment
• Architectural and engineering fees
• Contingency funds

These figures can usually be found without much difficulty in the "Jail" or "Corrections" section of the County Budget.

However, there are a number of other costs which may be more difficult to find and calculate, but which have a major impact on the total jail construction cost.

Financing Costs

The cost of financing a new jail usually appears as part of the County Budget's Proposed Capital Plan or Program. The most common method of jail construction financing is through the issuance of county bonds. The two factors which ultimately determine the long-term cost of financing will be the life of the bond, usually 20 or 30 years, and the annual interest rate to be paid to bond buyers. When financing costs are added to the costs of construction, total project costs can more than triple. For example, a 100 bed Jail for which construction costs are $4.3 million could cost the taxpayer $13 million before the bonds are paid off.

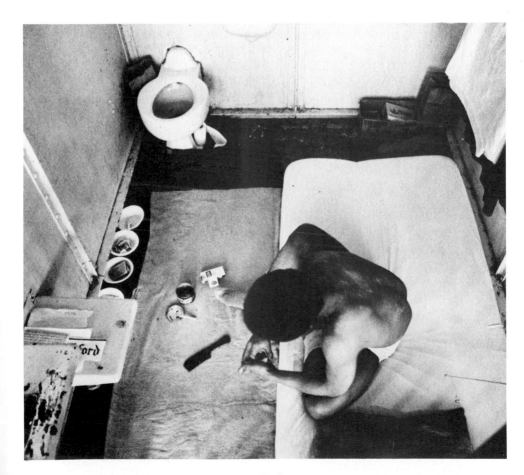

Inflation can cause significant cost overruns, particularly since many months or even several years can pass from the time the original estimates are prepared and a bid accepted, to when construction actually begins.

Once a total cost for financing and building the new or remodeled jail is determined, the figure is divided by the number of cells or bed spaces intended for the facility to determine the cost to build one cell or bed space.

Operating Costs

The U.S. Department of Justice's National Institute of Corrections estimated in 1980 that the average cost of housing one inmate in jail for one year is $14,000, with 70 percent of this amount for personnel, 10 percent for in-jail services, and 20 percent for maintenance and utilities. The operating costs of a jail, over the 30 year life of the jail, are usually 16 times the cost of constructing the jail.

In comparison, a study prepared for the National Council on Crime and Delinquency, which included not only these direct operating costs, but also added such societal costs as legal aid and the loss of taxes from inmates employed before incarceration, estimated that the average yearly cost of one inmate in a New York City jail totaled $40,668.

Estimated jail operating costs vary widely, depending upon the number of factors included in the calculations. There are, however, certain basic costs which are common to all calculations.

Staff costs include a portion of the salaries and wages of the sheriff and sheriff's deputies, and the total salaries and wages of all jail personnel, plus benefits and pensions for these employees.

In-jail services include the costs of food, clothes, laundry, linen, medical care, education programs, library service, exercise and recreation programs, and any staff time associated with these activities not included among regular jail personnel time.

Maintenance and utility costs include electricity, heating, sewage and garbage removal, water, telephone, plus maintenance, repair or replacement of equipment and supplies. This category also includes liability insurance costs.

To calculate the operating costs of the jail in your community, the basic source is again the County Budget and in particular its "Jail" or "Corrections" section. However, such costs as employee benefits and pension payments may be included in other sections of the County Budget, such as that on overall employee costs, and must be calculated from this total amount.

Once the total operating expenditures for the jail are determined, this figure should be divided by 365 days to determine the total operating cost per day. This total cost per day is then divided by the average daily population (or if the jail is overcrowded, divided by the design capacity) of the jail to determine the cost per inmate per day. This dollar amount, in turn, is multiplied by 365 days to find the cost to house one inmate for one year in the jail under consideration.

National Jail Costs

Calculating jail costs to the nation as a whole is difficult, given the complexity of the data and the lack of uniformity in the way in which they are collected.

However, some national estimates can be determined using the cost figures presented above.

According to the Bureau of Justice Statistics 1978 *Census of Jails,* the total number of jail beds in the nation was 261,166. Using the National Institute of Corrections average cost of housing one inmate for one year of $14,000, the total cost to the nation of filling those 261,166 beds for one year is $3.8 billion per year.

The Unitarian Universalist Service Committee's National Moratorium on Prison Construction estimates that as of January 1984 there were 85,440 jail bed spaces proposed or under construction. At its estimated average cost of $49,306 per bed space, the total cost to build all the jails presently planned is $4.2 billon.

Combining these estimates, the total cost to the nation to operate all current jails at capacity and to build all planned jails is $8 billion.

Alternative Forms of Financing Jail Costs

The soaring costs of jail incarceration have forced many local governments to explore alternative financing methods for jail construction and operation. A number of financing options are available to local governments including:

- **Lease/Purchase Option:** Funds for jail construction are obtained from private investors/firms. Governments agree to pay an annual sum for a specified number of years to lease a facility and assume ownership at the end of the lease period. In most cases the government retains control of the design, construction, operation and maintenance of the facility.

  A National Institute of Justice publication points out that "the most controversial aspect of lease/purchase financing is its use to circumvent the debt ceiling and referenda requirements of general obligation bonds. Because no voter approval is required, lease/purchase agreements undeniably reduce citizen participation in corrections policy."

  A variation on the lease/purchase agreement is for local governments to create a non-profit corporation to borrow the necessary funds for jail construction and then to lease the new jail from the corporation.

- **Charging inmates for room and board:** Under this system inmates are responsible for paying the costs of their terms of incarceration on a predetermined per-day basis. Inmate responsibility for room and board costs has been a component of many work release programs, both when operated from the jail or in a separate facility. Collection of fees is easier in work release systems, however, because inmates are employed and their paychecks are channeled directly through work release staff, who make the necessary deductions.

  Since most inmates have meager incomes prior to their incarceration, and are likely to be unemployed upon release, the feasibility of collecting incarceration fees is questionable. In some jurisdictions, inmates' financial situations are assessed at the point of intake into the jail and only those who are determined to have the ability to pay will be charged for their jail stay. If inmates are charged based on their ability to pay, legal questions of economic discrimination are raised. Additionally, administrative costs (collection, paperwork) may prove to be greater than the fees collected. State authorizing legislation may be required before local governments can undertake collection of inmate jail fees.

- **State Subsidies for County Jails:** Seventeen states provide subsidies for local corrections, for half-way houses and work release centers, for jail construction and/or training of personnel. Seven states have subsidy programs for jail construction to help bring the jails into compliance with state standards.

Jail Conditions and Use Of Standards

Jail Conditions

Jails vary greatly in size, type of physical plant, training of staff, inmate services, programs and available resources—from small rural jails to large urban jails.

In examining jails, U.S. Supreme Court Justice William J. Brennan, Jr., enumerated the following conditions which make up the totality of the jail, as stated in his concurring opinion in *Rhodes v. Chapman,* (1981):

- **Condition of the Physical Plant** (lighting, heat, plumbing, ventilation, living space, noise levels, recreation space);
- **Sanitation** (control of vermin and insects, food preparation, medical facilities, lavatories and showers, clean places for eating, sleeping and working);
- **Safety** (protection from violent, disturbed or diseased inmates, fire protection, emergency evacuation);
- **Inmate Needs and Services** (clothing, nutrition, bedding, medical, dental, and mental health care, visitation time, exercise and recreation, educational and rehabilitative programming);
- **Staffing** (trained and adequate guards and other staff, avoidance of placing inmates in position of authority over other inmates).

Most urban jails are crowded and plagued by the myriad of problems associated with crowding. Many small jails have major shortcomings. Here are some statistics on jail conditions in general:

- 47 percent of the 3,493 jails in the United States are more than 35 years old.
- Only 20* jails which have applied to the Commission on Accreditation for Corrections have been accredited as meeting standards for adult local detention facilities.
- More than 65 percent of all jails have only one staff person on duty—handling the telephones, dispatching, admitting, releasing and supervising the inmates.
- Only 38 percent of the jails have a doctor available on a regularly scheduled basis.
- Only 13 percent of the jails have facilities or services for the mentally ill and only 17 percent have services for alcoholics.
- Only 128 jails which have applied to the American Medical Association have been accredited for their health services.
- 81 percent of all jail inmates live in less than 60 square feet of cell space each, the accepted minimum standard; that is less than the size of two double bed mattresses.

In addition to these problems, a survey of sheriffs by the National Sheriff's Association cites personnel as the number one problem area confronting jails. Such personnel problems include lack of training, inadequate salaries (the average starting salary for a jail officer is $10,780 per year) and heavy staff turnover.

The second most significant problem identified by the sheriffs surveyed was the conditions in jail. Many jails are antiquated, poorly ventilated, substandard structures which do not meet minimal standards of fire protection, food service, health and sanitation.

*As of October 1985.

11

Use of Standards to
Improve Jail Conditions

One strategy for improving jail conditions is to enact and enforce jail standards. Standards developed by professional organizations such as the American Correctional Association and the National Sheriffs' Association, and by state legislatures are designed for use across the entire range of jail activities. Standards prepared by groups such as the American Medical Association and the American Bar Association are applicable primarily in those areas of the jail's operation which involve the unique concerns of those organizations. Standards developed by national groups are optional unless the jail is applying for certification by the association.

The effectiveness of state standards in improving jail conditions has been hampered by a number of factors. Some states have created voluntary standards. Other states have legally binding standards, but they do not have inspection programs, and even in states that do, enforcement can be lax or even non-existent. Finally, many localities lack the financial resources necessary to provide required improvements.

Legal Issues and Jails

Law suits against sheriffs, jail administrators and county commissioners have increased in the past ten years. Jails have been faced with suits challenging unconstitutional conditions of confinement, mistreatment of inmates, lack of due process, and inadequate supervision, to name some areas. In 1983:

- 10.7 percent of all jails were under court order to remove unconstitutional conditions of confinement.

- 19.9 percent were involved in a pending lawsuit over such issues as overcrowded conditions, lack of recreation, lack of programs, outdated facilities, and inadequate medical care.

- 70 percent of the 100 largest jails were under court order or in litigation involving conditions of confinement or crowding. Litigation in these 100 jails alone affects over 30 percent of the jail inmates in the nation.

Conditions of Confinement
and Inmates' Rights

In general, convicted inmates and pretrial detainees retain important constitutional rights despite their incarceration. As the Supreme Court noted in *Wolff v. McDonnell* (1976), "There is no iron curtain between the Constitution and the prisons of this country." (This and other court rulings apply to jails as well as prisons.)

These rights are founded in the Constitution and its Amendments: the First Amendment governing inmates' rights to freedom of speech, exercise of religion, access to the press, and right of correspondence; the Fourth Amendment governing an inmate's right to privacy and the issue of body searches; the due process clause governing access to the courts and to legal materials, and procedural due process; and the Eighth Amendment governing medical care and cruel and unusual punishment.

However, the legal status of pretrial detainees differs from that of convicted inmates. The constitutional provisions governing these two groups are therefore different. Two lines of Supreme Court cases establish the standard governing constitutional conditions: *Bell v. Wolfish* (1979) and *Rhodes v. Chapman* (1981).

In *Bell v. Wolfish,* the Supreme Court held that due process forbids the imposition of punishment upon unconvicted pretrial detainees, but noted that every condition of confinement does not amount to punishment. To show that a particular condition in punitive, inmates must show either an intent to punish, or that the condition is not "reasonably related to a legitimate governmental goal," such as internal order and security.

In 1984, the Supreme Court reaffirmed its holding in *Wolfish* and applied it to the issue of the denial of contact visitation to detainees and convicted prisoners at the Los Angeles County Jail. In *Block v. Rutherford,* the Court held that the denial of contact visitation was "reasonably related" to the jail's concerns about internal security and contraband; the Court reversed a lower court order granting contact visits to certain categories of inmates.

The Eighth Amendment ban on cruel and unusual punishment is the standard of review for the conditions under which convicted (sentenced) persons are incarcerated. In *Rhodes v. Chapman,* the Court held that double-celling of prisoners in 63 square foot cells in a modern, "unquestionably . . . top-flight, first class facility" did not amount to an Eighth Amendment violation. The majority opinion noted that conditions may amount to cruel and unusual punishment if they involve the "unnecessary and wanton infliction of pain," are "grossly disproportionate to the severity of the crime" or "result in the infliction of pain without any penological purpose." The Court continued, "Conditions . . . alone or in combination, may deprive inmates of the minimal civilized measure of life's necessities."

Justice Brennan's concurrence elaborated on the factors courts should consider in determining conditions violating the Eighth Amendment and formulated a test that has been widely followed in recent federal court decisions: "...a court considering an Eighth Amendment challenge to conditions of confinement must examine the totality of circumstances." Even if no single condition would be unconstitutional in itself, "exposure to the cumulative effect of prison conditions may subject inmates to cruel and unusual punishment...."

Medical Care

The standard governing the government's liability for medical care was set in the 1976 decision, *Estelle v. Gamble.* The Court held that "deliberate indifference to serious medical needs of prisoners constitutes the 'unnecessary and wanton infliction of pain'... proscribed by the Eighth Amendment."

Courts have held that jail inmates have the right to receive adequate and prompt medical care (including mental health care) of a quality comparable to that received by people outside of jail. Failure to provide this kind of care may expose the jail to damage liability. Screening on intake for communicable diseases has been required by some courts, as has adequate medical screening of intoxicated persons on intake and monitoring throughout the period of detoxification and withdrawal.

Personal Searches

A number of jail cases have addressed the practice of strip searching. A strip search is a search in which a person is required to remove all of his or her clothing. A body cavity search involves either a visual or manual inspection of the inmate's body cavities.

In *Wolfish,* the Court upheld a requirement that inmates submit to visual body cavity searches after contact visits. Noting that the Fourth Amendment only prohibits unreasonable searches, the Court articulated a balancing test between the "need for the particular search and the invasion of personal rights that the search entails. Courts must consider the scope of the particular intrusion, the manner in which it is conducted, the justification for initiating it, and the place in which it is conducted."

Courts have drawn varying conclusions about what constitutes reasonable strip search requirements for detainees and convicted inmates.

Courts have barred close visual inspection of anal and genital areas, while upholding the requirement that inmates strip. Courts have held that inmates must be given notice that they may be subjected to body cavity searches on less than probable cause. Strip searches without reasonable cause in connection with depositions, visits to the law library, transfers and medical visits have been pro-

hibited or limited. The courts have reached varying conclusions on the circumstances justifying strip searches of visitors.

Some courts have ruled that searches may only be conducted on pretrial detainees if there is reasonable belief that the detainee is carrying contraband or weapons, or will remain in the jail with other inmates overnight. A number of courts have awarded damages to persons arrested for minor offenses who were strip searched.

Protection from Inmate Assaults

The sheriff has a legal duty deriving from the Constitution and from common law tort principles to protect jail inmates from physical and sexual assault by other inmates. To sustain a constitutional claim, inmates must show the jailer's "deliberate indifference," "callous indifference," "gross negligence," "egregious failure to act," or "reckless disregard" for the inmate's safety and show that this conduct led to the assault, according to a number of court decisions.

Assaults are more common under crowded conditions and in jails with architectural blind spots which impede surveillance of the inmates in common areas or in cells which house more than one inmate. Without adequate supervision in inmate living areas, there may be nowhere an inmate can be secure. Courts have stressed the need for training of staff and adequate supervision of inmates to decrease the risk of assaults.

Jail Suicides

The Courts have ruled, in a number of cases, that jailers may be liable for inadequate custodial care of suicidal inmates if their actions amount to "deliberate indifference."

Equal Access

According to *Glover v. Johnson* (1979) and *Canterino v. Wilson* (1982), women must be provided the same access as men to all services and programs available in the jail under the Equal Protection Clause of the Fourteenth Amendment.

Litigation

Jail conditions litigation is often slow, time consuming, expensive and frustrating for all concerned. It is not unusual for cases to go on for years and trial and judgment do not usually end the case. Motions for modifications are made, negotiations are held, settlements arrived at and further orders issued. The court may appoint monitors to oversee compliance with the court order, a procedure that insures the most complete compliance with court decrees. Lack of resources by the jail or the county does not constitute a justification for maintaining unconstitutional facilities. Courts can and have ordered reductions in the number of inmates held at a facility or improvements in the conditions of confinement when Eighth Amendment violations were found.

Section 1983 of the Civil Rights Act of 1871 has also been applied by the Supreme Court to local governments. According to *Monell v. Department of Social Services* (1978), local jurisdictions are liable for money damages for constitutional violations and cannot employ a "good faith" defense to avoid damages, nor is a lack of funds to improve conditions a defense. Public officials have also been held personally liable under Section 1983, although they may make a good faith defense.

Jails which have avoided or minimized litigation against them usually follow written policies and procedures; have mandatory training for jail staff; provide good management, sanitation and health care; adhere to state jail standards; and use a classification system.

The classification system is used to assess jail inmates and identify those with special needs, such as juveniles, mentally ill and retarded people, those under the influence of or withdrawing from drugs or alcohol, and potential suicides. Separation of these individuals from the general jail population, provision of care and treatment, and/or diversion from the jail to appropriate social service agencies lessen the jail's risk of litigation and liability.

Jails vary in the variety of programs and services available, but in examining the constitutional adequacy of jails, the courts have called for: health and mental health services, drug and alcohol treatment programs, education, outdoor recreation, indoor activities, work activities, a law and general library, religious services, a canteen, a visitation program and work release opportunities.

Jail Crowding

One of the greatest problems facing many of our jails is that of crowding—too little space for too many people:

- 7,000,000 people, equal to three percent of the total U.S. population, pass through the nation's jails each year.

- 81 percent of all inmates live in less than 60 square feet of cell space each, the accepted minimum standard; that is about the size of two double bed mattresses.

- 11 percent of all jails are under court order to improve conditions and 20 percent are involved in pending lawsuits for such problems as crowded conditions, lack of recreation programs, outdated facilities and inadequate medical care for inmates.
- 45 percent of all the jail inmates are held in the country's 130 largest jails; these four percent of all jails hold an average of more than 250 inmates per day.
- the jail population has risen by one third during the last four years.

Jail crowding can be viewed as a primary cause of many other jail problems: health and safety problems, the incidence of rape, suicide and other violence, psychological stress among both inmates and jail staff, violations of Constitutional and other legal rights, lack of services and programs, and deteriorating physical plants, among other problems.

This is not to imply that building more jails is necessarily the solution to crowding and its related problems. The solution to overcrowded jails rests in the hands of many people—the courts, police, county commissioners, alcohol and mental health agencies and the community at large, among others. The jail is only part of a complex system, but the decisions or the lack of decisions of many others affect the jail population. The roles of these other officials and alternatives which reduce the jail population are discussed in other sections.

What is jail crowding? Jail capacity is measured in two ways, *rated* and *operational* capacity. Both of these terms are imprecise, nonstandardized and subject to various interpretations.

- **Rated capacity**—the number of inmates the jail was designed to hold.
- **Operational capacity**—the level of population at which the jail can function from day to day. This is usually a management decision made by the jail administrator. According to the Bureau of Justice Statistics, in many large jails operational capacity is defined pragmatically as the total number of inmates they are required to house, while in smaller jails it is defined as what they can effectively manage.

The Bureau of Justice Statistics' latest sample survey of the jail population on June 30, 1982 showed a national jail occupancy rate of 95 percent.

However, there are two major factors which are not taken into consideration in this figure. The first is "client flow" through the jail. Since the sample survey is for one particular day, it provides a "snapshot" of the jail population, which in reality is not static, but constantly changing. For example, the jail population was estimated to be 209,582 people on the census day of June 30, 1982, but it probably would have been higher during cold winter months and certainly would have been much higher on a weekend. During the 12 months prior to June 30, more than 7,000,000 people passed through the nation's jails.

Second, these estimates of capacity do not take into consideration the variety of jails in which this jail population is housed. According to BJS, the 100 largest jails in the nation hold 40 percent of the total jail population. The level of crowding and the problems caused by the size of the jail population in these large, primarily urban jails are distinctly different from those in smaller jails. For the large jails, the population exceeded rated capacity by four percent.

Smaller jails placed themselves at 92 percent of their operational capacity and at 80 percent of their rated capacity. It would appear that any unoccupied jail space in the nation is in these smaller jails.

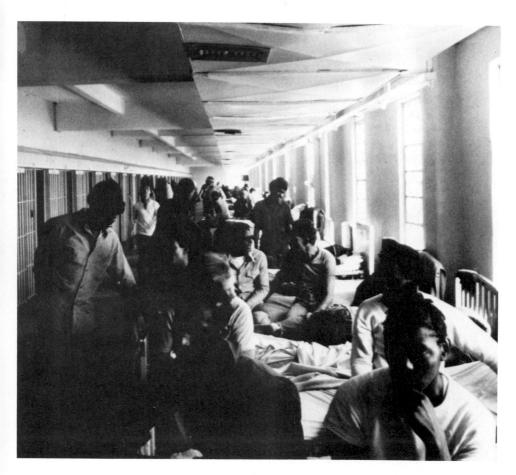

Another problem occurs in those jurisdictions where state prisoners are placed in local jails because the state prisons themselves are so crowded that no bed space is available. In 1983, the latest date for which statistics are available, jails in 18 states were holding 8,078 state prisoners in their cells due to the lack of state prison space.

In summary, there is no precise definition of what a "crowded" jail is. Your jail officials should be able to give you its rated and operational capacity, the average daily population, the recent peak population, and the average size of a cell (60 square feet per person is the national standard). From these figures you can get an indication of how crowded the jail is.

Reducing Jail Crowding

A number of different strategies are being used across the country to reduce jail crowding. Those based on diverting specific population groups are described in other sections of this book. The following are general strategies dealing with crowding.

Population Caps

In a few jurisdictions, judges have set an upper limit (cap) on the number of people the jail can hold. When that limit is reached, the jail is required to maintain that limit by releasing inmates according to various criteria.

In New York City, U.S. District Court Judge Morris Lasker in July 1983 ordered the release of 475 pretrial inmates due to crowding. He ordered the release of those with the lowest amount of bail ($1,500 or less) and within this group, those who had been in jail awaiting trial the longest.

Another method of release used by *prisons* with a cap on population is to release those sentenced inmates who are within 45 days of being released. Prison caps are usually legislatively mandated, while jail caps have been set by courts. Caps on prison populations also mean that state prisoners held in local jails remain there, thus further crowding the jail.

Solving the problem of crowding by looking at the end of the process is very difficult. Rather than looking at the exit from the jail, one might look at the entrance. (See the section on alternatives to jail for ways to reduce the population at entry into the criminal justice system.)

Building New Jails

Building new jails is exceedingly costly—an average of $43,000 for one new bed space, according to Bureau of Justice Statistics estimates, and an average of $5.77 million for a new facility, according to the Unitarian Universalist Service Committee's National Moratorium on Prison Construction.

21

Those who favor building claim new jails will provide needed space, will relieve problems associated with deteriorating physical plants, including costly litigation associated with poor jail conditions, low staff morale, lack of space for programs and services, and will provide an opportunity to meet the latest jail standards.

Those who oppose construction cite not only the heavy cost to the local taxpayers, but also claim that increased jail space often leads to "widening the net," that is, incarcerating people who would not be put in jail if unoccupied beds were not available. Such groups claim that ample jail space would be available if those who have been inappropriately jailed—such as juveniles, mentally ill and retarded people, public inebriates, and many non-dangerous minor offenders—were renovated from jail. They point out that jails do not rehabilitate people nor does putting more people in jail reduce the crime rate. They cite alternative punishments which they claim are more cost effective.

Women In Jail

Nearly half a million women are locked up in America's jails each year, according to the Bureau of Justice Statistics. On any given day, 13,500 woman are in city and county operated facilities, awaiting trial or serving short sentences. Many are charged with non-violent offenses and are not a danger to the community, but their limited financial resources make bail impossible. The women in jail tend to be poor, undereducated, young, and representative of minority groups in disproportionate numbers to the general population:

- 73 percent of the women in jail are under 30 years of age;
- 66 percent were unemployed before their incarceration;
- 58 percent lived on less than $3,000 a year and 92 percent had less than a $10,000 yearly income;
- 47 percent have one or more children dependent upon them;
- 58 percent have less than a 12th grade education;
- 54 percent are minorities;
- 64 percent are drug users, and 68 percent of these used drugs daily before they entered jail;
- 59 percent are awaiting arraignment or trial; they have not been found guilty of the crimes with which they are charged.

22

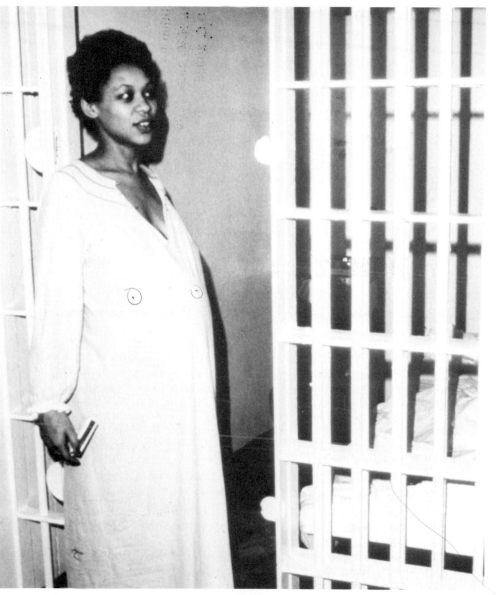

Many women are in jail for victimless crimes such as prostitution. A 1981 study of women in the San Francisco jail found 40 percent of the women in jail were charged with prostitution, 30.3 percent with property crimes (theft, shoplifting, forgery, fraud), 12.1 percent with drug offenses, and 6.1 percent with violent offenses.

Problems Specific to Women

Women in jail live under the same conditions as do men, but in addition they face the problems of unequal access to services. Women, perhaps due to the small number in jail (6.5 percent of those in jail), rarely have the same access as men to recreation, education, work release and vocational education programs, when such programs exist in the jail. When there are occupational training programs in the jail, women are often limited to training in beauty care, sewing, cooking and other traditional, low wage occupations instead of the better paying jobs for which men are trained. Lack of past employment experience outside the home often prevents women from qualifying for a work release program position.

Women are also confronted by many problems specific to their gender. Many women in jails are mothers with sole responsibility for the support of their children. Separated from their children, they live in fear of losing custody of their offspring to the state. Many jails do not permit children to visit their mothers in jail or severely restrict those visits. There is a lack of gynecological care for jailed women and seldom any special health care for pregnant women; use of contraceptive pills is often interrupted because they are not available in jail.

Alternatives to Jail and Improved Services

Alternatives to incarceration specifically designed for women and improved services for women in jail are available in some communities. Among these are:

- **Diversion Programs:** Community work service programs where women offenders perform a specified number of hours of unpaid community service instead of serving their time in jail.

- **Pretrial Release with Bail:** A revolving bail fund is maintained by community organizations and used to post bond for female pretrial detainees in selected cases.

- **Crisis Intervention:** Programs that begin working with women at their first encounter with the criminal justice system, providing crisis intervention services to attempt to divert unsentenced women from jail. Services include assisting women to deal with judges, attorneys, bail bondsmen, probation officials, relatives and friends; arranging for temporary shelter for the women's children; contacting employers and family members; screening women for diversion to mental health facilities when appropriate; individual and group drug and alcohol counseling; and job readiness training. Supportive services following the women's release are also available including employment, training, education, housing, financial assistance, and child care.

- **Services for Women in Jail:** Community organizations, using professionals and volunteers, offer a wide range of services for women in jail, including job training and counseling. Volunteers also act as advocates for women in jail, providing a link with their families and enhancing communication with the criminal justice system. Many programs also provide follow-up services to women following their release from jail, such as job placement, help in locating housing and arranging for day care for their children, and referrals to drug or alcohol treatment and counseling.

- **Visits with Children:** Some jails provide a supervised play area for children of jailed women off the main visiting room or permit mothers to play with and feed their children during visits.

- **Work Release:** In some jails, women have equal access to work release programs that allow them to work during the day and return to the jail in the evening. In some jurisdictions, work release is operated out of a separate facility where children are allowed to stay with their incarcerated mothers in an apartment-like setting. The mothers receive job training during the day, while the children attend school or are in day care. Another option for mothers in a work release program is to return to their homes during the day to care for their children.

Juveniles In Adult Jails

In 1980, the Juvenile Justice and Delinquency Prevention Act was amended by Congress to require that states participating in the act remove all juveniles from adult jails by 1985. In spite of federally funded efforts to remove juveniles from adult jails, the Bureau of Justice Statistics 1982 *Survey of Jail Inmates* reported 1,700 juveniles in adult jails on the day of the survey, the same number as reported four years earlier. According to BJS, this works out to more than 300,000 juveniles having been held in adult facilities during the 12 months prior to the BJS survey.

In most states, juveniles are persons who have not reached age 18, but in a few states juvenile status ends with the 16th birthday. The initial impetus for the development of the juvenile court in 1899 was to provide special protections and remove children from jails and other parts of the adult criminal justice system. In many jurisdictions, however, children are still facing confinement in adult jails.

In 1982, for the first time, a federal judge ruled that the existence of the juvenile justice system, with its goal of individualized treatment, precludes the placement of juveniles in adult jails. Juveniles, it was ruled, had a due process right to be free from pretrial punishment.

In the case, *D.V. v. Tewksbury,* (1982), the U.S. District Court in Oregon ruled that "to lodge a child in an adult jail pending adjudication of criminal charges against that child is a violation of that child's due process rights under the 14th Amendment to the United States Constitution."

Of the 300,000 youths who spend time in our nation's jails each year, nearly 25 percent are accused of status offenses—truancy, running away from home—acts which if committed by adults would not be a crime. Only 10 percent of the juveniles in adult jails have been charged with violent crimes. Two-thirds of the juveniles held in adult jails will be released at their court hearing.

In adult jails, juveniles can fall prey to adult offenders, being raped or assualted or educated in criminal behavior. Rarely is there enough staff for adequate supervision to guard against physical or sexual assaults. When attempts are made to separate juveniles from adult offenders, the juvenile often ends up in the isolation cell. Alone, many attempt suicide. For every 100,000 juveniles placed in adult jails, 12 will commit suicide. This is eight times higher than the rate of suicide in secure juvenile detention centers.

Why Juveniles Go to Jail

The reasons that communities have had difficulty in removing juveniles from jail include:

- a lack of specific release/detain criteria (i.e., objective intake screening);
- a lack of alternative services, programs, and transportation to them;
- state statutes which allow detention of juveniles in adult jails;
- community disagreements over the type of alternatives needed and an overreliance on a secure juvenile detention facility as the solution.

Alternatives to Jailing Juveniles

There are processes and alternatives to jailing juveniles that protect the rights of the juvenile, as well as the safety of the community. Most of the following are far less costly than the use of cell space in an adult jail:

27

- **Use of Objective Criteria:** Objective written criteria detail the reasons a juvenile should or should not be held in secure detention. Criteria can include offense, legal status and legal history and are used in determining the type of supervision that a juvenile requires while awaiting a court appearance.

- **Twenty-four Hour Intake Services:** Detentions and jailings can be reduced substantially through the availability of 24-hour detention intake screening services. Intake services provide immediate screening, counseling, referrals to services and make case-by-case release or detention decisions using objective criteria.

- **Use of Summons or Citations:** When the police arrest a juvenile, instead of taking him or her to jail, they may issue a ticket/summons/citation. The juvenile is released to his or her home and notified when and where to appear in court.

- **Emergency Shelter Services:** Emergency shelter services provide temporary residential placement for youths who do not require locked security, but who are unable to stay in their homes or who do not have homes. Emergency shelter services can be provided in a variety of ways, including programs specifically created to provide emergency services, group homes, runaway shelters that are capable of meeting crisis needs, or licensed "host homes" in the community.

- **Runaway Programs:** Runaway programs are variations on group residences that specifically serve runaways or children who have been forced to leave home. These programs provide short-term residential care followed by referrals for long-term care as needed.

- **Home Detention:** Home detention programs permit juveniles to reside in their homes under daily supervision from a caseworker, pending their court appearance. The caseworker also provides added supervision for the juvenile during the court process.

- **Group Home Detention Programs:** Group homes are generally community residences used to house between 7 and 12 juveniles. A group home detention program provides its residents with counseling, adult supervision and an alternative living situation.

- **Family Crisis Intervention Programs:** Trained counselors provide intervention services to juveniles and their families who are in crisis. Services may include counseling, training in problem solving skills, enrollment or re-enrollment in school, homemaking assistance and financial planning, as well as referrals to other services. These programs focus on family problems rather than just the problems of the juvenile and provide short-term services on a 7-day, around-the-clock basis.

- **Community Advocate Programs:** Community advocate programs are a variation on home detention programs. Community advocates are adults who spend a number of hours a week with juveniles who are in trouble. In one-to-one relationships, the ad-

28

vocate functions as a positive role model, friend, problem solver, authority figure and provides supervision and guidance.

- **Transportation Services:** The provision of transportation can be vital to keeping young people out of jail. It may be necessary, particularly in rural areas, to travel long distances to transport juveniles to appropriate detention facilities or to alternative placements. Cooperative agreements between intake specialists and law enforcement officers have been developed in several communities to provide transportation for juveniles to a community that has the appropriate services.

- **Secure Juvenile Detention Program:** A small number of juveniles require secure custody. Secure juvenile detention programs provide the structure and supervision by trained staff that those juveniles require. The primary goal of secure detention is to hold juveniles temporarily in a secure setting pending adjudication or placement in another program. Services are directed toward basic physical needs, education and constructive use of time. Counseling services are often provided.

- **Comprehensive Juvenile Services Center:** Comprehensive juvenile service programs offer highly structured, intensive day treatment programs that provide supervision in education, recreation, vocational training, drug and alcohol counseling, as well as individual and family counseling, for a juvenile who resides at home. This type of program alleviates the fragmentation that characterizes social services programs.

Public Inebriates and Jail

One out of every ten arrests in the United States is for public intoxication, a total of more than one million arrests every year. (This does not include the 1.4 million arrested for drunk driving—see separate section on this.) In some areas, 20–40 percent of those in jail are there only for public drunkenness. In many localities, people arrested for public intoxication are placed in jail to "sleep it off."

29

Suicides by intoxicated people in jail are a great problem. In one study, some 85 percent of those who committed suicide in jail were intoxicated at the time of death.

The costs of arresting, booking, jailing and trying these individuals are well over $400 million per year, a major drain on the scarce resources available to the criminal justice system. Holding them in jail takes up already crowded jail space which could be used to hold those charged with more serious crimes. In states where public intoxication has been decriminalized, people drunk in public are still being arrested—but now they are charged with disorderly conduct, littering or disturbing the peace.

The issues of holding those arrested only for public intoxication in the costly, high security jail also apply to a related jail population group, public inebriates.

Needs of Public Inebriates

A public inebriate is someone who is repeatedly drunk in public, has frequent contact with the police, often resulting in incarceration, and has limited financial or other resources. Public inebriates are usually chronic alcoholics who have no job, no home, no family. Many have been jailed literally hundreds of times. A public inebriate, in contrast to a drunk driver, does not operate a motor vehicle and is generally not a danger to society.

The majority of public inebriates are in desperate need of health and rehabilitation services which they cannot get in jail; 62 percent of all jails have no doctor available on a regularly scheduled basis and 83 percent have no alcohol treatment services. In a sample study of more than 3,000 public inebriates in New York, 20 percent had bone fractures, 50 percent had wounds, cuts or burns, 20 percent had hallucinations, 20 percent suffered from severe brain damage, 20 percent had severe gastrointestinal bleeding, 15 percent had cardiopulmonary problems, and 25 percent had indications of seizure disorder.

Alternatives to Jail

Alcohol services and programs already available in the community are usually more cost effective than arresting, booking, arraigning and detaining public inebriates in jail. The following are the kinds of services that can benefit public inebriates and decrease the burden on the criminal justice system:

Shelters and Reception Centers provide basic human needs such as food, a bed, clean clothing and referral to other appropriate services. While shelters may not get at the underlying problem of public inebriation, they save on jail costs and serve as the entry to services which can help to rehabilitate the public inebriate. Costs in shelters are as low as $10 a day—compared to the average jail cost of $40 a day.

Detoxification Services are designed to assist the individual's safe withdrawal from alcohol by providing health care, counseling, short-term living quarters and outpatient treatment. Ninety percent of public inebriates need only a non-medical, social detoxification setting to sober up, while the remaining 10 percent require medical detoxification. After they have sobered up, ongoing alcohol services can be provided.

Extended Care may consist of in-patient, residential treatment, halfway houses, aftercare and out-patient services. These programs allow the individual to stabilize physically, psychologically and socially and provide the support necessary for the person to successfully reenter his or her community.

Domiciliary Care is long–term residential care for the chronic public inebriate with extreme physical and psychological needs. Domiciles provide a range of services for those who because of age, years of poor nutrition and medical care may never be able to return to the community as productive members.

Housing, Support and Job Training are long–term solutions to the problem of the public inebriate, most of whom need assistance in locating permanent housing and training that will result in gainful employment. These services are usually available through various programs in each community. However, the public inebriate requires special guidance in order to take advantage of them.

Transportation Services can ensure that the public inebriate is taken to alternative treatment services. This type of system allows law enforcement officers increased time to handle serious offenders.

Drunk Drivers
and Jail

Drunk drivers pose a special threat to community safety. Federal, state and local governments, and community groups have pursued methods of reducing the numbers of people who drive under the influence of alcohol, including:

- public awareness campaigns;
- encouraging citizens to report drunk drivers;
- raising the legal drinking age;
- using law enforcement check points to stop and test all motor vehicle operators for alcohol content level;
- specialized patrols;
- increased prosecution of driving-under-the-influence/driving-while-intoxicated cases;
- videotaping drunk drivers to increase the likelihood of court conviction;
- sentencing drunk drivers to community service work in hospital emergency rooms;
- listing the names of all convicted drunk drivers in local newspapers;
- suspending or revoking the drivers' licenses;
- sentencing more drunk drivers to jail;
- sentencing drunk drivers to longer jail terms.

Since 1981, 34 states have enacted tougher penalties against drunk drivers, 25 of which involve mandatory jail terms. How these new laws affect jail populations remains to be demonstrated. Data on the numbers of drunk drivers in local jails are still in the process of being collected and tabulated.

The National Institute of Justice's report, *The Impact of Mandatory Confinement on Criminal Justice Operations,* which examines the effects of the new drunk driving laws in five jurisdictions where a jail sentence is mandatory, will be released in late 1984. The National Highway and Traffic Safety Administration plans to fund a study in 1985 which will examine the impact of jail sentences on the recidivism rate of drunk driving offenders.

Even without statistical studies to confirm increased jail populations due to the increased incarceration of drunk drivers, the impact of these laws is acknowledged in communities across the country. Many jail administrators report that they have backlogs of people convicted of drunk driving waiting to serve their time in jail, when space becomes available. Some communities are building special new jails for drunk drivers, but critics argue that putting drunk drivers who are often middle class people in a special, usually better, facility discriminates against the minor, usually poor, offenders being held in the regular jail.

Although only preliminary data are available, it seems obvious that mandatory jail terms for drunk drivers do increase the size of the jail populations. Additionally, special weekend sentences, which are often being used for drunk drivers, serve to increase jail populations at times when jails are traditionally crowded.

Suicides In Jail

In 1980, the National Center on Institutions and Alternatives (NCIA) conducted one of the few comprehensive studies of suicides in jail. Its report, *And Darkness Closes In, National Study of Jail Suicides,* showed that the suicide rate for adults in jails is 16 times greater than for the general population.

NCIA surveyed 16,909 jails and lockups (temporary holding facilities) and identified 419 suicides which occurred during 1979. Demographic data collected on 344 of the 419 suicides provides a clearer picture of jail suicides:

- More than 50 percent of the suicide victims took their lives during the first 24 hours of incarceration, with 27 percent of the suicides occurring within the first three hours.
- 73.6 percent of the suicide victims were charged with non-violent crimes. Alcohol/drug related charges accounted for more than 30 percent of the charges.
- Almost 60 percent of the suicide victims were under the influence of alcohol and/or drugs at the time of incarceration.
- Two out of every three inmates who committed suicide were being held in isolation, where they were placed for their own protection or for surveillance.

- 67.3 percent of the suicide victims were white.
- 96.5 percent were male. (This can be attributed to the small numbers of women in jail.)
- Almost 75 percent of the suicide victims were 32 years old or younger.
- 53.3 percent of the victims were single.
- 91.4 percent of the suicide victims were unconvicted at the time of their deaths.
- 95.9 percent chose hanging as their method of suicide.

The NCIA study also reported significant relationships among intoxication, isolation, and length of incarceration as factors in jail suicides. Over 88 percent of the inmates who commit suicide under the influence of alcohol and/or drugs at the time of their confinement committed suicide within the first 48 hours of incarceration, and over half of these victims were found dead within the first three hours of confinement. Of the inmates in isolation who committed suicide, 63 percent did it in the first 48 hours and 30 percent of these were in the first three hours.

Methods to Deter Potential Suicides

Jail suicides can be reduced through a variety of changes in the jail structure and system:

- Development of a written plan to prevent suicides, with which all jail personnel are trained.
- Screening on intake by trained booking officers to identify potential suicide risks.
- Diversion at intake of likely candidates for suicide, who do not require secure confinement—such as intoxicated persons (drug/alcohol), the mentally ill, and juveniles—from jail to appropriate social services.
- Increased training for jail staff in identifying and supervising potential suicide victims.
- Eliminating the use of isolation cells for potentially suicidal inmates.
- Constant supervision by staff, volunteers or specially trained inmates of potential suicides in special observation rooms or cells.
- Holding *all people* for the first 48 hours in cells with other inmates and where they are closely supervised by staff.
- Design changes to prevent suicides, such as barless windows and doors, blankets and bedding that tear away under pressure, television monitors and cell design that provides easy sight and sound supervision.
- Removing inmates' belts and shoe laces for 48 hours.

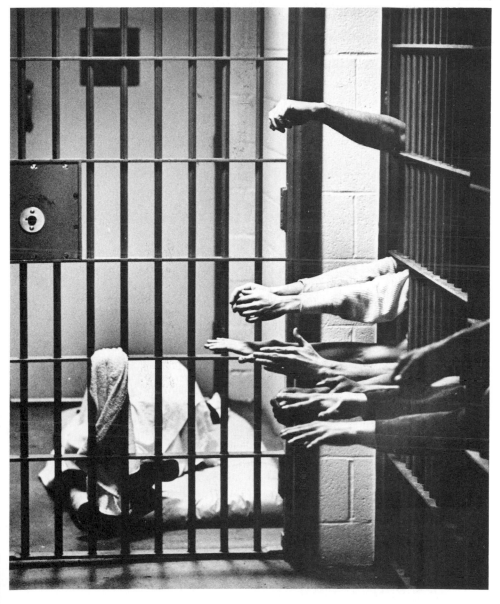

Jails Operated by Private Companies

A newly proposed alternative to the traditional financing, owner-ship and operation of the jail by local government is the privately owned and operated jail. Contracting for jail services, such as food, health care and other programs, is not a new idea for the criminal justice system, but only recently has this concept been expanded to include private ownership and operation of the entire jail.

Although the federal government has begun contracting with private firms to operate low security holding facilities for illegal aliens, and privately run training schools and treatment centers for juveniles have existed for a number of years, jails have generally remained under the total authority of sheriffs and local government.

It is understandable why local government officials, faced with crowded, antiquated jail facilities and lawsuits or court orders, might be ready to consider turning over the entire jail operation, and all its problems, to some other authority. However, the concept of privately operated and owned jails has yet to be tested and evaluated. During 1983 and 1984, at least 10 private-for-profit companies have gone into business to build and operate private jails, although as of July 1984, none is yet operating a jail.

Suggested Benefits of Private Ownership

A number of reasons have been suggested for turning over jail ownership and operation to private companies:

- The private sector may be able to build and operate jails more cost effectively, more efficiently, and with greater flexibility.
- Funding for new jails may be easier to obtain, since voter approval of general obligation bonds would not be necessary.
- Much of the bureaucratic "red tape" may be eliminated in a privately operated jail system.
- Privately operated jails could be administered by a Board of Directors, who would ensure that standards are complied with. Compliance with standards would decrease the costs of liability insurance.

- Private-for-profit companies could offer profit-sharing to its jail employees as a fringe benefit, in order to recruit better qualified personnel.
- Employee training costs are tax deductible for private companies. This would act as an incentive for private vendors to provide training to jail personnel.
- Private companies may be able to bring greater innovations to the correctional field.
- Using a private company, a county could experiment with a new model of corrections without making a permanent commitment to it.
- It may be easier for a private contractor to develop a regional jail because it is not hampered by the political considerations of the public sector.
- Governmental contracts with private companies can be renegotiated on a yearly basis, thus providing local governments with some leverage should the private vendor fail to meet any contractual obligations or operate the jail in an unsatisfactory manner.
- Private companies pay taxes on their profits, thus providing a return to taxpayers.

However, a number of legal, contractual and ethical issues remain unresolved. Among them are:

Contractual and Legal Issues

- How, by whom and at what cost would privately owned and operated jails be monitored for contract compliance? How would legal requirements be enforced?
- How would legal liability be divided between the local government and the private company when a suit is brought against the jail?
- Many states now reimburse or subsidize local governments for certain jail expenses. How would this be handled in the case of a privately owned and operated jail?
- Would private company jail employees be eligible for state or federal correctional training now given to local government jail employees?
- Who would be responsible for maintaining security and providing services if private company jail personnel go on strike?
- Would a private company have a right to refuse to accept certain inmates at its jail? if so, where would they be detained?
- If the privately run jail reaches the contractual limit on the number of inmates it is to serve, what happens to those who continue to be sentenced to jail?
- What would happen if the private jail company went bankrupt or out of business?
- The major costs of jail operations are staff salaries, yet the average starting salary for a jail employee is only $10,780 per year.

Could a private company lower the cost of jail operations without reducing these salaries or reducing the number of jail employees? Would a reduction in the number of employees reduce jail security?

- The public presently has certain rights of access to the jail as a public facility. How would these rights be affected by private ownership and operation?
- Would state and local jail standards and regulations, which apply to jails owned and operated by local governments, apply to privately run jails?
- Once having given up jail ownership and operation, what are the options for a local government which is unsatisfied with the private contractor's operations, performance or costs? Will the local government have become dependent on the company?

Ethical Issues

- Depriving a person of his or her liberty has traditionally been a sanction imposed only by the State. Should the enforcement of this sanction be delegated to a private company?
- What would be the public's attitude about permitting profit to be made by a private company through depriving people of their liberty?
- Is it appropriate for a private company to impose conditions of maximum security, including the possible use of deadly force?
- Will governments use the private financing of jails to circumvent debt ceilings and referenda requirements of general obligation bonds and thus reduce citizen participation in corrections policy and control of their tax monies?
- Will government officials expect privately owned and operated jails to solve problems that are the product of other parts of the criminal justice system?
- Elected sheriffs and other local officials have traditionally been accountable to the public for the jail. Would this public accountability be diminished if a private company owns and operates the jail?
- If a local government contracts to pay a private company to hold a certain number of inmates, is there any incentive for the local government to reduce unnecessary or inappropriate confinement or to seek less costly alternatives to incarceration?

Alternatives To Jail

There are a number of points in the criminal justice system where alternatives to incarceration are possible.

- **Pretrial release** allows the individual freedom from custody pending trial.
- **Pretrial diversion** is an alternative to prosecution or arrest. In general, charges are dismissed after a defendant successfully completes the requirements of the diversion process.
- **Sentencing options** are non-jail punishments for those who have been convicted.

The use of alternatives to jail, for both those people awaiting trial and those convicted of crimes, varies from community to community. Most jurisdictions use some of them—although the extent varies enormously. However, as our jails become more and more crowded, communities are increasingly examining non-jail options to determine which are underutilized in their criminal justice processes.

Pretrial Release Options

The purpose of pretrial detention is to assure the defendant's appearance at trial. For someone who has not yet been tried—and thus is presumed innocent—jailing is a harsh option when less severe choices are available. Therefore, pretrial release alternatives to jail are used by many communities to reduce pretrial detention. In addition:

- Pretrial release can reduce the crowding in jails and free up space for more serious offenders, thus reducing the need for new construction.
- Pretrial alternatives can cost less than jail incarceration.
- Persons held in jail awaiting trial are less able to participate in their defense and are more likely to receive jail sentences than those who are released awaiting trial, all other variables being equal.
- Pretrial release reduces the discrimination against the poor inherent in detaining people only because they cannot make bail.
- Pretrial release enables the individual to maintain employment and family support while awaiting trial.

At the various stages in the criminal justice process from first contact with law enforcement officers to disposition of a case, a number of decisions are made that can result in the release of the individual. For example, a police officer can issue a field citation at the scene of an incident, a law enforcement official can release a person on his or her own recognizance after booking at the stationhouse, or a judicial officer can set different types of bail at a judicial hearing.

The stringency of the option chosen and the conditions set for release are usually in direct proportion to the severity of the charge and the possibility of the person's non-appearance at trial. The

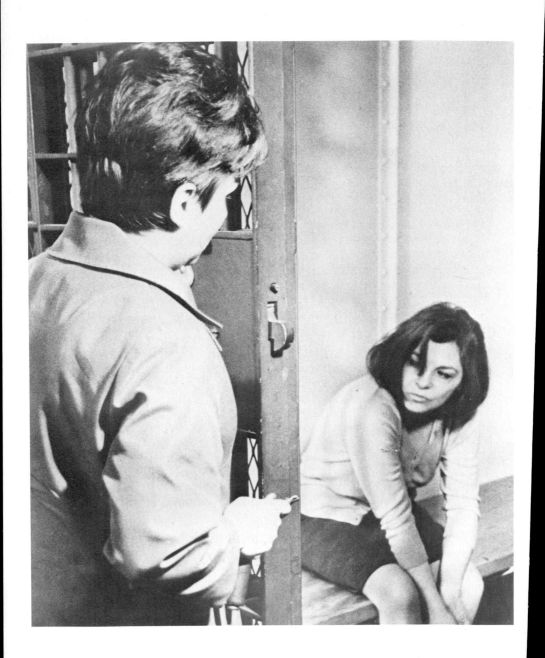

number of defendants who deliberately do not appear for trial typically does not exceed four percent of all released defendants.

The pretrial release options described below are in an increasing order of stringency.

Non-Financial Release Options

- **Summons or Citation**—The arrestee is given a summons by the police officer to appear in court to face charges. This reduces the costs of arresting and booking the defendant.

- **Stationhouse Release**—Stationhouse release generally refers to release on personal recognizance authorized by personnel at the booking facility shortly after an arrestee is booked. Stationhouse release affords a more extensive check on an arrestee's background than a field citation, but also avoids the costs of jailing.

- **Release on Recognizance**—Release on recognizance, or release on own recognizance (ROR; OR) refers to release of a defendant who meets certain criteria, on his or her promise to appear. The criteria include employment history, prior record, and community ties. ROR implies no additional conditions of release other than that the defendant, who meets the criteria for release, promises to appear in court as required.

- **Conditional Release**—Conditional release refers to a form of non-financial release in which the defendant is required to meet specified conditions during the pretrial period. These conditions may include checking in with a pretrial release agency, maintaining a specified place of residence, staying away from complaining witnesses, etc.

- **Supervised Release**—Supervised release means there is more frequent and intensive contact between the pretrial release agency or supervising agency and the defendant than in conditional release. For example, the defendant may be required to participate in counseling, attend a drug abuse treatment program, or work with vocational counselors to secure employment.

- **Third Party Release**—In third-party release, another person or organization assumes the responsibility of assuring that the defendant will appear in court. Third party releases may involve release to the custody of a parent, relative, or other individual, or to an organization, such as a halfway house or treatment program.

Financial Release Options

- **Unsecured Bail**—Release on unsecured bail is similar in practice to release on recognizance, except that a bail amount is set by the court for which the defendant may be held liable should he/she fail to appear.

- **Deposit Bail**—Deposit bail, also known as 10 percent bail, differs from surety bonds (see below) in that the defendant or the defendant's friends or family deposits a specified portion of the face value of the bond (often 10 percent) with the court. At the disposition of the case, the defendant receives back most of the amount deposited, less an administrative fee (generally one to three percent of the face value of the bond), thus providing a source of revenue to the courts at minimal cost to the defendant.

- **Cash Bail**—Cash bail requires that the defendant post the full amount of the bail bond to secure release. The money posted is returned to the defendant following disposition of the case, provided the defendant appears as required.

- **Surety Bail**—Surety bail is an arrangement under which a private bail bondsman posts bail for the defendant—in effect, providing a loan to the defendant. It is at the discretion of the bondsman whether or not to post bail for any given person, and there is a charge (ranging from 5 to 20 percent of the face value of the bond) for the bondsman's services. This amount is not refunded to the defendant. Should the bondsman wish to prevent loss of his or her money (or that of his or her insurance company), he or she must return the defendant to court himself or otherwise collect the funds from the defendant. In many instances, bail bondsmen will require that the defendant post collateral for the loan in the form of property or other assets.

- **Property Bail**—In some jurisdictions, the defendant may post property or other assets in the place of cash.

The Bail Bond Controversy

When financial conditions of release are set, the amount of bail a person must post to be released from custody is usually set by a judge or through a predetermined bail schedule that assigns a specific dollar amount for certain charges. The defendant can then either post the full amount or pay a bondsman a percentage of the bond as a non-refundable fee. For example, if a person has bail set at $10,000, he or she might pay a bondsman $1,000, plus collateral if the bondsman requires it. Whether the person is found innocent or guilty, makes all court appearances or not, the defendant does not get any of the $1,000 back.

In return for the fee, the bondsman is liable to the courts for the full amount of the bail if the defendant does not appear in court.

This system has been the source of controversy for several years. The most common criticism is that it discriminates against the poor. (Fifty-seven percent of the people in jail awaiting trial remain there because they cannot afford bail. One third of these cannot afford even $125 in bail.) Those without substantial liquid assets remain in jail, while wealthier individuals are set free.

The second major criticism is that the bail system effectively removes the pretrial release decision from the judge and gives it to the bondsman. A judicial decision is transferred to a profit motivated enterprise. When a judge sets a low bail, the intention is usually to release the defendant. But a bondsman may consider the fee to be earned on a low bond too small to warrant the effort. Conversely, a judge may set a high bail with the intent of keeping the defendant incarcerated, but a wealthier individual may have no trouble paying the bondsman's fee and obtaining release. This has been especially troubling in the cases of defendants with alleged connections to drug smuggling and organized crime.

Another problem, opponents of the bail system contend, is that bondsmen do not generally pursue defendants who flee. Most bondsmen rely on the police to rearrest a defendant who does not appear in court.

Some bondsmen, though, employ "bounty hunters" to track down defendants with exceptionally large bail who flee. In many states, where the court has released the defendant to the bondsman under a private contract, the bondsman and his employees have the authority to take exceptional measures to insure the defendant's appearance if the defendant has fled: they can enter a defendant's home without a warrant, cross state lines with the individual, and detain the defendant without any sort of hearing.

The bail controversy has been fueled in recent years by a number of scandals involving payoffs by bondsmen to judges, jailers, court clerks and others. The American Bar Association, the National District Attorneys Association and the National Legal Aid and Defender Association, among others, have called for the elimination of bonding for profit. The state of Kentucky has outlawed it and a number of other states have virtually eliminated it by implementing a variety of other pretrial release alternatives, most notably deposit bail.

Proponents of the bonding system claim that it is a legitimate business, that it reduces the number of defendants who flee and that it decreases the pretrial population in jails. They indicate that abuses involve only a small number of bondsmen and that these problems are best dealt with by establishing standards of operation and self-policing of these business enterprises.

Pre-Trial Diversion

For some people arrested by the police, diversion from the criminal justice system may be more appropriate than prosecution. For example, the intoxicated person who needs alcoholic counseling services, the mentally ill person who needs mental health services, or the juvenile who needs help from the social service system—may be diverted from the criminal justice system to the appropriate agency. Such diversion may be done by the police, the pretrial agency, the prosecutor, or the court (which may suspend prosecution on the condition that the person accept social services.)

A more detailed description of these programs and processes is in the sections on these groups.

Post-Conviction Options

For the person who has entered a plea of guilty or been convicted through the trial process, there are a number of sentences or punishments which can serve as alternatives to jail time or reduce the time a person is incarcerated. Depending on the type of sentence, they are administered by the local probation department or specialized community agencies. These include:

- **Fines**—These are the most commonly used alternatives to incarceration. Many believe that their use could be vastly expanded; others claim that they discriminate against those least able to pay and are an inadequate punishment for the wealthier "white collar" criminal.

- **Restitution**—This alternative requires the offender to repay the victim for property stolen or damage incurred. Restitution program staff monitor the payment schedule. These programs often assist the unemployed offender to find a job to ensure that repayment can be made.

- **Probation**—To control or help defendants with a problem that may have led them into crime, probation is often given as an alternative to jail. The defendant is required to maintain contact with the probation department and to use the alcohol, drug or other social service referrals the department provides. Restitution, community service, or participation in a drug, alcohol, mental health or employment program may be made a condition of the probation.

- **Community Service**—Punishment by community service requires that the offender perform an unpaid service for the community for a specified period of time under supervision.

- **Intensive Supervision**—This is a specialized probation where the offender is seen as often as daily by a case manager who monitors the offender's behavior and compliance with court ordered conditions, such as restitution, job search or drug treatment.

- **Client Specific Planning**—For a fee, a specific alternative to jail sentencing is developed for the individual offender and presented to the judge. The plan is tailored to specific problems of the offender and includes restitution, punishment and conditions placed on the offender.

- **Shock Probation**—This type of sentence does not eliminate jail time, but couples a short jail term (the "shock")—often on weekends—with a period of supervised probation.

44

- **Work or Study Release**—Individuals with this type of sentence work or study during the day and are jailed in the evenings and on weekends. Participants in these programs are spot-checked while at work or school and are usually housed in minimum security facilities, which are less costly than jailing.

As with pretrial alternatives to jail, most communities use some of these post-conviction alternatives, but they are often underutilized for incarcerated persons. Most communities rely heavily on detention and few use all of these alternatives in an integrated plan to reduce the number of people who are filling crowded jails.

One drawback to these alternatives is that they may be used to extend the reach of the criminal justice system to even more people. Those who in the past would have been given a verbal reprimand, may now be formally processed through an "alternative to jail" program, while the jail remains filled with the poor, the unskilled and the socially dysfunctional. To avoid this, alternative programs should be designed for those already in jail or those defendants most likely to receive jail sentences.

Contributing to Solutions:
The Community and the Criminal Justice System

The jail is not the sheriff's or jail administrator's responsibility alone. The sheriff or administrator does not control who goes to jail or how long they stay. Even when the jail has reached its "rated capacity" and still more people are sent to it, the sheriff or administrator usually cannot refuse to house them.

In addition to the crime rate, the actions of judges, prosecutors, defense attorneys, local and state elected officials, pretrial release agency staff, police, social service agency staff, and the community at large all affect the jail population. Since the cell capacity of the jail is limited, all these elements together must plan how it is to be used. Individually, each component can also have an impact on the jail population. The following are ways in which various groups and individuals in the criminal justice system and in the community can contribute to solving the complex problems of the jail.

45

State Legislators

- Establish community corrections acts which encourage community alternatives to jail.
- Fund local community mental health programs and other social services to meet the needs of special jail population groups.
- Enact laws giving police the authority to use citations/summons for misdemeanors.
- Enact state jail standards, with enforcement mechanisms, and provide financial assistance to counties, attempting to comply with the standards.
- Decriminalize various victimless crimes.

Local Elected Officials
County Commissioners, City Council Members, Mayors

- Encourage all components of the criminal justice system to work together to reduce the reliance on jail incarceration as a sanction.
- Design programs and allocate funds for social service programs to meet the needs of troubled populations who often wind up in jail due to a lack of services.
- Establish a planning group which included representatives from all parts of the criminal justice system to look at all sides of the problem.
- Establish a pretrial release agency and provide the option of 10 percent bail.

Judges

- Make greater use of alternatives to incarceration for appropriate individuals.
- Make greater use of pretrial release where appropriate.
- Release people who would otherwise be in jail and place restrictions on their activities.
- Ensure faster court processing of pretrial detainees.
- Avoid weekend sentences when the jail is usually more crowded.
- Release defendants, where appropriate, into the care of a qualified person or organization.
- Ensure 24 hour, 7-day-a-week availability of magistrates for release decisions (night courts for those arrested on the weekends or at night).
- Divert persons with special problems, such as the mentally ill or the public inebriate, to community treatment programs.

Police

- Increase the use of citations or summons for minor offenders.
- Divert persons with special problems, such as the mentally ill or the public inebriate, to community treatment programs.

Prosecuting Attorney

- Recommend alternative sentences such as community service or restitution in appropriate cases.
- Expedite screening and processing of court cases, particularly where defendants are awaiting trial.
- Ensure speedy processing of mental disability cases.

Public Defender

- Expedite appointment of a public defender, particularly in cases of pretrial detention.
- Recommend to the courts alternatives to incarceration for misdemeanors.

Pretrial Release Agencies

- Recommend greater use of release on own recognizance, 10 percent bail and conditional release.
- Provide sufficient staff to interview all defendants and develop recommendations for release/detention.
- Expedite processing of release recommendations to the court.
- Reduce recommendations of "release only on money bail" which can adversely affect the poor.

Probation Officer

- Expedite the processing of presentence reports to reduce the period of incarceration between trial and sentencing.
- Become aware of the alternatives to incarceration and recommend greater use of alternatives for appropriate individuals.

Court Administrators

- Implement court management systems (i.e., computerized court systems) that expedite the handling of court cases.
- Provide a 24-hour intake person who, using objective criteria, will screen out people who are inappropriate for jail confinement (e.g., juveniles, mentally ill) and refer them to alternative placements.

Sheriffs/Jail Administrators

- Keep judges informed on a daily basis of the population of the jail.
- Take a leadership role in bringing together all parts of the community and criminal justice system to develop ways to reduce the crowding.
- Request the legislature to make changes in laws, pass enabling legislation and promote state/county partnerships to solve jail problems.

Social Services Programs

- Ensure that services are available to homeless alcoholics/public inebriates who would otherwise end up in jail.

- Ensure that local detoxification programs will accept people brought in by the police.
- Provide 24-hour emergency services for the mentally ill and accept referrals from the police.
- Provide training to law enforcement personnel in identification and referral of mentally ill, mentally retarded persons who come in contact with the police.

Community

- Visit the jail to see how many people are in it, for how long, for what offense. Educate other citizens.
- Establish a planning commission to look at the problems of the jail and make recommendations.
- Encourage community organizations to study the criminal justice system.